BRANCH LINE TO HAYLING
including the Isle of Wight Train Ferry

Vic Mitchell and Keith Smith

in association with

Alan Bell

Other books from Middleton Press

BRANCH LINE SERIES
Vic Mitchell & Keith Smith

BRANCH LINES TO MIDHURST
BRANCH LINE TO SELSEY
BRANCH LINES TO EAST GRINSTEAD
BRANCH LINES TO ALTON
BRANCH LINE TO HAYLING

SOUTH COAST RAILWAY SERIES
Vic Mitchell & Keith Smith

BRIGHTON TO WORTHING
WORTHING TO CHICHESTER

OTHER BOOKS
INDUSTRIAL RAILWAYS OF THE SOUTH-EAST
Chalk Pits Museum
WAR ON THE LINE
Bernard Darwin
GREEN ROOF OF SUSSEX
Charles Moore
MIDHURST TOWN – THEN AND NOW
Vic & Barbara Mitchell

STEAMING THROUGH KENT
Peter Hay

Published to commemorate the 21st anniversary of the closure of this much loved branch.

First published 1984.

ISBN 0 906520 12 6

© *Middleton Press, 1984.*

Phototypeset by   CitySet Ltd, Chichester.

Published by   Middleton Press
Easebourne Lane
Midhurst, West Sussex.
GU29 9AZ

Printed & bound by   Biddles Ltd.,
Guildford and Kings Lynn.

Cover: A typical scene at Havant in the 1930s, before the rebuilding of the station. The Terrier is on the loop line and is about to run round the coaches of the branch line train. (Dr. J.C. Allen)

CONTENTS

ACKNOWLEDGEMENTS

Our grateful thanks go to the photographers shown in the caption credits and also to M.G. Trigg and the Portsmouth Reference Library. Many of the tickets have been provided by Alan Bell ; much darkroom work has been undertaken by D. Dornom and M.J. Grainger; proof reading has been done by Mrs. E. Fisk, J. Hanwell, N. Stanyon; our wives have helped in so many ways; the railwaymen of the branch were so co-operative with Alan Bell – our appreciation is expressed to them all.

GEOGRAPHICAL SETTING

Hayling Island is composed of sedimentary deposits of mainly clay, with some gravel and sand. The terrain is almost flat and is part of the coastal plain between the Selsey Peninsula and Portsea Island. The southern shore is of sand, appealing to holidaymakers, but the remainder of the coastline borders the mud of Langstone Harbour to the west and Chichester Harbour to the east. The island remained isolated from the mainland until linked by a frail bridge in 1824. This gave the inhabitants access to the small market town of Havant, located just above the flood plain, at the east end of Ports Down. Agriculture and tourism were the principal industries, the latter booming after World War II with the construction of three large holiday camps. The population of the island was a little over 1000 when the railway opened and showed a 50% increase by the end of the century.

HISTORICAL BACKGROUND

The road bridge to the island was acquired in 1851 by the Hayling Bridge and Causeway Company who were also empowered by Act of Parliament to build a railway from the main coast line of the London, Brighton & South Coast Railway at Havant (opened in 1847), to the harbour at Langstone, at the north end of the bridge. This line never materialised.

The London & South Western Railway arrived at Havant in 1859 with its direct line from London and interest in a branch to Hayling was revived. The Hayling Railway Company was formed in 1860 by local business people and they obtained Parliamentary Powers in July of that year. To attract further capital, another Act was obtained in 1864 which permitted a southward extension and docks to be built.

This map is reproduced from Trigg's Guide to Hayling Island published in 1892. It was based on an earlier Ordnance Survey map on the scale of 1" to 1 mile which shows clearly the limited extent of the isolated communities.

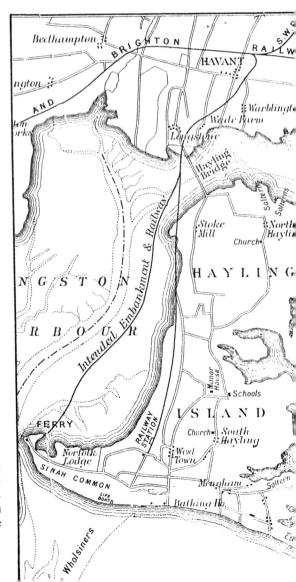

The line was opened from Havant to Langstone on 19th January 1865, but then the company ran into difficulty. In order to avoid the expense of buying land on the Island for the line, it had been decided to construct an embankment on the mud flats in the sheltered waters of Langstone Harbour. Unfortunately, the area was not as sheltered as the company directors imagined and the bank was severely eroded before the railway could be completed. Work commenced in 1867 on a land based route, under the guidance of a new board of directors and company chairman, but with the same contractor – Frederick Furniss.

The Board of Trade inspector was invited to pass the line fit for passenger traffic, but refused to do so as he found that the original part of the railway by then had many rotten sleepers and also an unauthorised level crossing at Langstone. The former was quickly remedied but the latter never was. The new section of the route was also unacceptable having been laid unevenly on beach shingle with inadequate signalling. A final complaint was "broken rails"! These matters were resolved in time for trains to run on the second day of Hayling Races – 17th July 1867 – the terminus being known as South Hayling. During the following winter the line had to be closed for repairs to flood damage at North Hayling.

Until the end of 1871, train services were operated on behalf of the company by Mr. Furniss, the contractor for the construction of the line. Thereafter an agreement was made with the LBSCR to provide the train

service. This arrangement lasted until 1922, when the company was absorbed by "Big Brother". There had been an earlier suggestion that the LSWR should operate the line, providing a direct link with London by means of a bridge over the coast line, but this was never to be.

The coming of the railway brought a number of incidental benefits to the island. For example, from 1872 the LBSCR allowed the public to use its telegraph system which was connected to London Bridge and other large stations. In 1877 a gas works was opened on a site close to the station, since the railway was able to provide cheap transport of coal. The arrival of the line also meant low cost carriage of island exports. These included oysters, salt and bricks, the latter by the million for the construction of the houses of West Worthing.

In 1883 work started at Langstone on the construction of a train ferry terminal and by August 1885 it was ready for the paddle steamer "Carrier" to provide a service, for goods wagons only, to the Isle of Wight. The thrice-weekly passage ceased in March 1888 and is more fully described elsewhere in this album. The harbour steadily silted up and regular goods traffic ceased in 1890.

The history of Hayling has revolved round weak bridges. The only locomotives permitted on the railway bridge were the Terriers but the heaviest vehicle allowed on the timber road bridge was 6 tons 6 cwt, which necessitated the use of small, special light-weight buses. In 1954 the limit was further reduced to only 5 tons and no bus was allowed to carry more than 13 passengers on the bridge – the others had to walk over, regardless of the weather. These limitations had a beneficial effect on railway revenue but

Route diagram showing the curve radii in chains and the gradient profile.

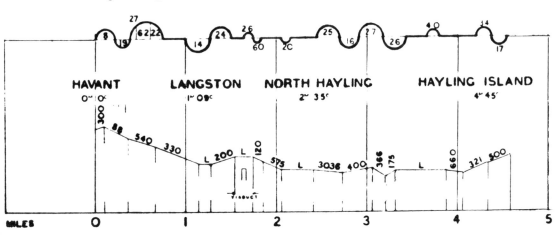

this advantage was lost to some extent when the new road bridge was opened in 1956. British Railways had inherited the right to impose tolls for the use of the road bridge and levied them until 11th April 1960, although they were collected on behalf of the Hampshire County Council from the beginning of 1955.

Unlike many branch lines in the early 1960s, the Hayling line was showing an operating profit, but the timber bridge linking it to the mainland was in need of replacement at an estimated cost of £400,000. After the inevitable objections had been swept under the carpet, the last public train service was operated on 2nd November 1963. After the closure, a scheme was announced to erect overhead wires and operate electric tramcars on the branch, but it came to nothing, partly due to the need to provide a bridge for the proposed Havant bypass.

Demolition of the bridge and lifting of the track started in 1966 and today the only structure standing is the terminal goods shed. The stumps of the bridge trestles and the timber piles of the train ferry berth and the old wharf are still visible.

TRAIN SERVICES

Mr. Furniss initially provided six return trips on weekdays only between Havant and South Hayling, departures being between 7.10 am and 6.30 pm. This was soon reduced to four journeys, with a shorter working day of 8.20 am to 4.35 pm. Neither Mr. Furniss or the company directors appear to have notified Bradshaws, publishers of the railway timetable for all Britain, of the existence of the line.

The LBSCR started with only four trains each way, but gradually increased this to ten by the end of the century, with nearly as many on Sundays. A similar frequency was operated until the SR was formed.

The SR was soon providing a summer service of fifteen weekday journeys, with seven on Sundays. In the summer of 1938, 17 trips were made on weekdays (with an extra train for cinema-goers at 10.47 pm from Havant on Wednesdays and Saturdays) and 15 on Sundays.

A frequent service was still maintained during World War II as the holiday-makers had been replaced by service personnel.

1. Miss Mabel Crassweller, photographed in 1918, when employed as a porter at Hayling Island. One of her duties was to travel to North Hayling each day to sweep out the waiting room. (H. Crassweller collection)

Nationalisation in 1948 brought little change to the timetable – 15 on weekdays, nine on Sundays and an extra on Saturdays. Winter reductions were made, especially on Sundays.

The booming sixties brought further increases of frequency – the final summer timetable showing 15 journeys on Mondays to Fridays, 24 on Saturdays and 21 on Sundays.

LOCOMOTIVES

One of the attractions of the branch to railway enthusiasts and casual onlookers alike was the apparent quaintness of the locomotives, due to their small size in relation to the coaches. Their diminutiveness was due to the weight restriction of the bridge, limiting it to carrying nothing heavier than the Terrier class locomotives of 28 tons 5 cwt. This class (A1) had been designed by Stroudley and built between 1872 and 1880. They were rebuilt by L.B. Billinton from 1911 onwards to class A1X. In view of the long and varied history of many of the locomotives that have worked the Hayling branch we offer a selection of potted histories of some of the better known and much loved machines of the last years of the line, together with the story of some of the unusual earlier engines. The two digit number shown is the one that was usually used in conversation, as the SR prefix B6 or 26 to the LBSCR number and the later BR prefix 326 was normally ignored by those working and travelling on the line. In 1957 a P class tank was unsuccessfully tried and later plans were made to upgrade the line for M7 tanks to be used, but were not put into action. All the seven Terriers surviving today on private railways have operated on the branch for various lengths of time.

No.2

Early life. Built in Hatcham Iron Works, Peckham, London, by George England & Co as an 0–4–0 T, with 2ft 10in diameter driving wheels, it was constructed around 1860, a few

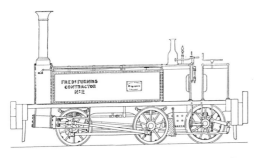

years before the famous England survivor *Prince*, which is still running on the Ffestiniog Railway.

Hayling life. It was used during the construction of the line by Mr. Furniss, the contractor, who added an odd-looking pair of 3ft diameter trailing wheels, presumably to give it more stability when it was used to provide the initial passenger services. His engine no. 1 was a Hawthorn 0–4–0 ST and he also used a 2–4–0 tender engine for some time.

After life. No. 1 and no. 2 were both sold to Mr. Boulton of Ashton-under-Lyne, a dealer in second-hand engines, who named them *Brighton* and *Portsmouth* respectively.

No. 115

Early life. Built as a 2–4–0 T by Sharp Stewart & Co of Manchester in 1869, it was initially numbered 96 by the LBSCR who set her to work on their Kensington branch. In 1872 she was fitted with a cab, transferred to

the Kemp Town branch in Brighton and named *Kemptown*.

Hayling life. In June 1874, she was allocated to Portsmouth shed, renumbered 115, renamed *Hayling Island* and operated the branch for 15 years. In 1877 she was again renumbered, 359, and in 1886 she became no. 499. See photograph no. 83.

After life. The company's locomotive engineer, William Stroudley, decided to give her a pair of trailing wheels and the inspection saloon illustrated above. The hybrid was not completed until after his death in 1889 and was withdrawn in 1898, the engine having had five different numbers and three different names! (E.R. Lacey collection)

No. 53

Early life. This 2–4–0 T was also a Sharp Stewart product. It was an export reject when purchased by the LBSCR in 1873. After use

on the Kensington line as no. 53, it was sent to Newhaven where it bore the name *Bishopstone* and the no. 270. The gong seen in this photograph could be used where the line ran along the public highway.

Hayling life. Following the success of no. 115, *Bishopstone* was sent to the branch in May 1878 and renamed *Fratton*. She was renumbered 357 in 1880 and 497 in 1886.

After life. Sold for scrap for £164 to George Cohen & Sons, in October 1890.
(E.R. Lacey collection)

No. 496

Early life. Purchased new from Kitsons for £1140 in December 1868, it was numbered 76

and worked on different parts of the LBSCR system.

Hayling life. It appears to have worked on the branch in the 1889-91 period when numbered 496.

After life. It worked local services from Eastbourne before being withdrawn in April 1895. (E.R. Lacey collection)

No. 40

Early life. Completed at Brighton Works in March 1878, her claim to fame is clearly seen on her side tank. An early member of class

AI, she became class AIX in 1918 when fitted with a larger boiler. She spent many years on the Isle of Wight where she became no. W11 *Newport*.

Hayling life. She was moved from that island to this in 1947, where she ran as SR no. 2640 until becoming BR no. 32640 upon nationalisation in 1948. She was painted BR black at Eastleigh in 1951 and worked the branch until its last year.

After life. Following closure, the engine became a static exhibit at Butlins Holiday Camp, Pwllheli. After this Welsh sojourn, the Isle of Wight Steam Railway acquired her for restoration to working order.
(E.R. Lacey collection)

No. 46.

Early life. Like many other Terriers it started its working life on London suburban services. Built in 1876, it was numbered 46 and was sold for £500 in 1903 to the LSWR for use on its Lyme Regis branch, carrying their number 734. In 1913 it was hired by the

Freshwater, Yarmouth & Newport Railway and bought by them two years later. During her use by the Southern Railway on the Isle of Wight, she acquired the number W8 and was named *Freshwater*.

Hayling life. From 1949 until the end of services, she was a frequent worker of the branch, as BR no. 32646.

After life. She was bought by the Hayling Terrier Fund for £750. She was later sold to Mr. Charles Ashby of Droxford (see our *Branch Lines to Alton*) and in May 1966 was displayed, as illustrated, outside the *Hayling Billy* public house. In June 1979, Whitbreads donated her to the Wight Locomotive Society and after 105 years was returned to traffic on the Isle of Wight. (A.A.F. Bell)

No. 50

Early life. Another creation of Brighton Locomotive Works in 1876 and named *Whitechapel*. It had a varied career before being shipped to the Isle of Wight in 1930, where it became no. W9 *Fishbourne*. Returning to the mainland six years later, it was renumbered 515S and became a shunter at Lancing Carriage Works. During 1946, it was oil-fired due to a coal shortage.

Hayling life. It displaced no. 32659 in 1953 as it had the larger coal bunker fitted for Isle of Wight service. It ran as no. 32650 and hauled the last scheduled passenger train from the island.

After life. It was purchased to serve as an exhibit in the Civic Centre of Sutton, but circumstances allowed it to be maintained temporarily in running order on the Kent & East Sussex Railway, and it has remained there ever since, as their no. 10 *Sutton*.

No. 55

Early life. From its introduction in 1875, it worked widely over the LBSCR network, bearing the now famous name of *Stepney*.

Hayling life. Records show that it was regularly operating the branch from 1926 onwards, although it appeared elsewhere on the Southern from time to time, and BR continued to shed it at Fratton for use on the Hayling line until April 1960.

After life. It operated the last BR passenger train on the Kent & East Sussex line in 1954 and was sold to the Bluebell Railway in working order in May 1960 for £750, including two coaches. This event marked the beginning of standard gauge railway preservation.

No. 70

Early life. Of 1872 construction, this engine served the LBSCR as *Poplar* until 1901 when it was sold to the independent Kent & East Sussex Railway, who also had frail bridges and a need for light-weight engines. It became their no. 3 *Bodiam* and ran until 1931, when it was merged with parts of their other Terrier to form an almost fresh engine.

Hayling life. BR took over the K & ESR in 1948 and after that line's closure to passengers in 1954, sent the engine to Fratton, bearing the number 32670. It then regularly worked on the branch, including hauling the last train.

After life. It was purchased by Mr. Wheele and returned to the K & ESR where it has again been running as no. 3 *Bodiam*.

No. 72

Early life. It was the first member of the class to enter service and the first to be sold. The sale was in 1898 and was to the Newhaven Harbour Co. She was given the name *Fenchurch* when built in 1872 but lost it in 1913. The Harbour Co. was acquired by the SR in 1926 and the locomotive was given the lowest number then vacant in the Terrier series, 2636. It was mostly used at Newhaven for the next 35 years.

Hayling life. She appeared briefly in August 1961 and ran regularly from late July 1963. As BR no. 32636 she was selected to haul the last special train on 3rd November 1963.

After life. She was an early arrival on the Bluebell Railway, in April 1964, where she had her name restored and also celebrated her centenary. In 1975 she took part in the locomotive cavalcade at the 150th Anniversary of the Stockton and Darlington Railway.

No. 78

Early life. An 1880 product which received the name *Knowle* and operated widely (including Hayling in the 1890s) until the SR sent her to the Isle of Wight, having her number changed from 678 to W4. She was soon named *Bembridge* and became W14. In 1936, she was sent to Eastleigh and condemned.

Hayling life. A new boiler was found for her and she arrived on the branch, looking like new, in 1937, bearing the no. 2678. Soon after nationalisation, in 1948, BR sent her to the K & ESR, where in 1949 she was derailed into a swamp near Wittersham Road. She was still running goods trains there in 1958 before returning to Fratton for Hayling services.

After life. After withdrawal in 1963, she was sent for display at Butlin's Minehead Holiday Camp. Eventually she returned onto rails for restoration on the West Somerset Railway and was subsequently sold to Resco Railways Ltd. at Woolwich.

LOCOMOTIVE SHEDS

In the early years of the line a small shed, with a water tank, was located close to the point where the present A27 road crosses the former route.

In 1874 a shed and pumphouse were erected at South Hayling, to the west of the platform. This shed, which had originally been at Petworth, was closed in 1894, being demolished a few years later. Thereafter, the branch engines were shedded at Fratton and brought over each day, sometimes with empty coaches.

When Fratton Depot closed in 1959, the engines continued to stand there overnight, as it was the signing on point for locomotive crews. All maintenance work then had to be carried out at Eastleigh.

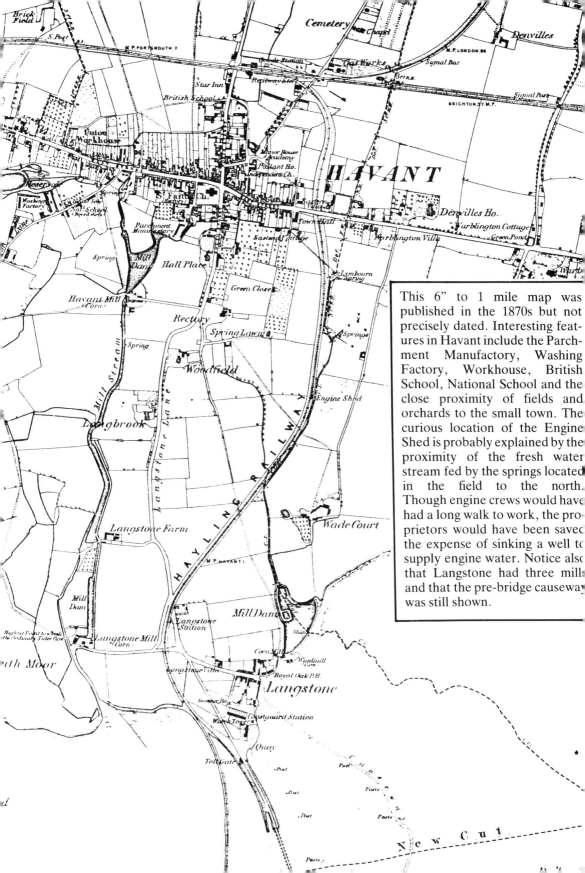

This 6" to 1 mile map was published in the 1870s but not precisely dated. Interesting features in Havant include the Parchment Manufactory, Washing Factory, Workhouse, British School, National School and the close proximity of fields and orchards to the small town. The curious location of the Engine Shed is probably explained by the proximity of the fresh water stream fed by the springs located in the field to the north. Though engine crews would have had a long walk to work, the proprietors would have been saved the expense of sinking a well to supply engine water. Notice also that Langstone had three mills and that the pre-bridge causeway was still shown.

8. The exterior of the south side of the original station, as seen in 1879. The buildings were demolished ten years later to make way for a new station. The only building to survive was the refreshment room, seen on the left. This lasted until the third station was erected in 1938. (Railway Magazine)

The 25" scale map of 1909 shows the proximity of the cattle market to the station. Cattle traffic was an important part of railway business for nearly a century and that was why the market was often so situated.

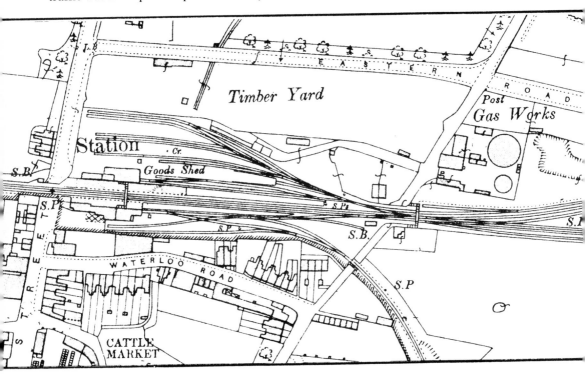

9. The interior of the second station, looking towards Brighton, with a train from Hayling in the bay platform. Notice that branch line passengers were given no weather protection but passengers changing main line trains had a completely enclosed footbridge.
(E. Jackson collection/Lens of Sutton)

10. Looking towards Portsmouth from the footbridge we obtain a fine view of the goods yard and staff on the right and the Hayling bay on the left. The word DANDO above the signal box roof was the trade name of the Littlehampton firm of Duke and Ockenden and is on one of their wind-driven water pumps. Students of railway signalling will find no less than nine semaphores in this view. No water column was provided for up trains as they would have started with full tenders at Portsmouth.
(National Railway Museum)

RAILWAY STATION HAVANT .22

11. One of Stroudley's Terriers, no. 43 *Gipsyhill*, waits to depart for Hayling with an immaculate train. Seldom does a photograph convey the splendour of the coach builder's skill so well. What magnificence it was for a mere branch line guards brake van! Later these vans included passenger compartments. Notice the engine admirer, the sedentary couple and more publicity from D and O at the base of their creation. In the distance we see the first level crossing on the branch and on the platform, oil lamps still exist, these were shortly to be converted to gas. (E.R. Lacey collection)

9351
SOUTHERN RAILWAY.
Issued subject to the Bye-laws,
Regulations & Conditions in the
Company's Bills and Notices.
H.M.F. on LEAVE.
Havant to
HAYLING ISLAND
Third Class
NOT TRANSFERABLE
SOUTHERN RAILWAY.
H.M.F. on LEAVE.
Hayling I.
Havant
Hayling Island to
HAVANT
Third Class
9351

12. The rear of the Hayling train carries an LV board. This was placed on the last vehicle of the train to indicate to signalmen that the train was complete. Before the advent of continuous brakes and track circuiting, vehicles shed accidentally on a journey could remain undetected with potentially disastrous results. Subsequently, a white painted rear lamp has served this purpose. In the distance is the North Street level crossing and the West Signal Box. These were lost in the 1938 rebuilding, together with North Box on the former LSWR line. Less obvious is the water tank (above the coaches) and the goods shed (behind the up platform). (Lens of Sutton)

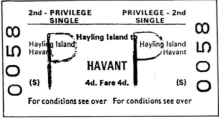

2nd - PRIVILEGE
SINGLE

PRIVILEGE - 2nd
SINGLE

0058

Hayling Island to

Hayling Island
Havant

Hayling Island
Havant

HAVANT

(S)

4d. Fare 4d.

(S)

0058

For conditions see over   For conditions see over

2nd - SINGLE

SINGLE - 2nd

17840

Hayling Island to

Hayling Island
Havant

Hayling Island
Havant

HAVANT

(S)

1/3   Fare 1/3

(S)

17840

For conditions see over   For conditions see over

13. Another of the many Terriers to appear in this album – *Preston*, after being re-numbered to 663 in 1913. The number plate is wooden, although the originals were cast in brass. Note the end windows and spoked wheels of the guards brake. (O.J. Morris/ Lens of Sutton)

14. The siding commencing under no. 53 was added about 1889 and was probably required for the transfer of vehicles to and from main line passenger trains. Such transfers would include horse boxes and vans for perishable commodities. The previous map shows that the branch connection faced Brighton and precluded direct running from the main line to Hayling. Later photographs reveal the layout revision that took place at the time of the electrification of the coast line in 1938 (Dr. I.C. Allen)

15. This 1930 view shows the Hayling Island line on the right and its connection to the main line in the centre. The grounded coach body behind the new water tower was a cheap way of providing accommodation for railway staff. (R.C. Riley collection)

16. During the reconstruction, a temporary wooden platform was provided for branch line trains for a period. The work was carried out in 1937-38 and included a provision of four tracks through the station (two being for non-stop trains), and a toilet for the signalmen (at the top of the steps). Close examination will reveal many other interesting details. (National Railway Museum)

17. SR no. 2661, formerly named *Sutton* by the LBSCR, waits at the new extended but yet unsurfaced platform. The coaches are ex-LSWR non-corridor stock. The line next to the warehouse was known as Leggett's siding. (Lens of Sutton)

HAVANT and HAYLING ISLAND

(timetable, 1938)

1938

19. During World War II the Southern Railway employed many female guards. Here we see Miss Molly Smith still at work in 1946. The driver is Percy Osborne who had to ignore the deplorable condition of no. 2659 in those days of austerity. (A.A.F. Bell)

18. The competitor waits outside the station. Southdown took over local services in 1926 and introduced these 26-seater Leyland Cubs ten years later. They were slow and often crowded but to many locals the bus service was geographically more convenient. Don't miss the railway detail and the brief telephone number in the background. (A.A.F. Bell collection)

20. The un-numbered engine was a migratory visitor calling in at Havant for refreshment. It was no. 30583 on its last journey on BR, in July 1961, travelling from Eastleigh to its new home on the Bluebell Railway, where it is now preserved. It had been built in 1885 for use on the LSWR suburban services and by 1919 had found its way onto the East Kent Railway, part of the Col. Stephens empire. The SR bought it in 1946 for use with two other survivors of the class on its sharply curved Lyme Regis branch. This is the first view in this album of a Terrier fitted with a tool box and a spark arrester (S.C. Nash).

21. The direct line to London can be seen swinging to the left beyond the footbridge. The route indicator above the down platform signal could show W for Waterloo, B for Brighton or H for Hayling. Branch excursion trains from the north or east would arrive and depart from this platform. A vestige of the bay platform remains today – as far as the ramp – having been shortened in 1972. (D. Cullum)

Miles	Down		Mondays to Fridays																Saturdays			
		am	am	am	am	am	am	pm	pm	pm	pm	pm	pm	pm	pm	pm		am	am		am	am
										K												
—	Havant .. .. .. dep	6 30	7 34	8 15	9 12	10 35	11 35	12 35	1 35	2 20	3 35	4 46	5 33	5 20	7 20	3 34	..	6 30	7 34	..	8 15	9 14
1	Langston	6 34	7 37	8 18	9 15	10 38	11 38	12 38	1 38	2 23	3 38	4 49	5 36	5 23	7 23	8 37	....	6 34	7 37	....	8 18	9 17
2¼	North Hayling	..	7 41	8 24	9 22	10 42	11 42	12 42	1 42	2 27	3 42	4 53	5 40	5 27	7 27	3 41	..	..	7 41	....	8 22	9 24
4½	Hayling Island .... arr	6 43	7 47	8 28	9 28	10 48	11 48	12 48	1 48	2 33	3 48	4 59	5 46	6 33	7 33	8 47	....	6 43	7 47	....	8 28	9 30

Down		Saturdays—continued																			
	am	am	am	am		pm	pm	pm	pm	pm	pm	pm	pm		pm	pm	pm	pm		pm	pm	pm	pm
Havant .. .. .. dep	10 5	1035	11 5	1135	..	12 5	1235	1 5	1 35	2 5	2 35	3 5	3 35	..	4 5	4 35	5 5	5 35	..	6 5	6 35	7 35	8 38
Langston	10 8	....	11 8	....	..	12 8	....	1 8	....	2 8	....	3 8	....	..	4 8	....	5 8	....	..	6 8	6 38	7 38	8 41
North Hayling	1012	..	1112	..	..	1212	..	1 12	..	2 12	..	3 12	..	..	4 12	..	5 12	..	..	6 12	6 42	7 42	8 45
Hayling Island .... arr	1018	1045	1118	1145	....	1218	1245	1 18	1 45	2 18	2 45	3 18	3 45	....	4 18	4 45	5 18	5 45	....	6 18	6 48	7 48	8 51

Down		Sundays																				
	am	am	am	am		pm	pm	pm	pm	pm	pm	pm	pm		pm	pm	pm	pm	pm	pm	pm	pm	pm
Havant .. .. .. dep	10 5	1035	11 5	1135	..	12 5	1235	1 5	1 35	2 5	2 35	3 5	3 35	..	4 5	4 35	5 5	5 35	5 6	6 35	7 5	7 35	8 5
Langston	10 8	....	11 8	....	..	12 8	....	1 8	....	2 8	....	3 8	....	..	4 8	....	5 8	....	6 8	....	7 8	....	8 8
North Hayling	1012	..	1112	..	..	1212	..	1 12	..	2 12	..	3 12	..	..	4 12	..	5 12	..	6 12	..	7 12	..	8 12
Hayling Island .... arr	1018	1045	1118	1145	....	1218	1245	1 18	1 45	2 18	2 45	3 18	3 45	....	4 18	4 45	5 18	5 45	6 18	6 45	7 18	7 45	8 18

The up service of this 1963 timetable appears under picture no. 28.

23. No. 46 and crew pose on 7th September 1963 alongside the small coal stage at Leggett's siding. This was staffed by a fire lighter/cleaner from Fratton, when the time-table required the turn-over engine to wait at this end of the branch. (A.A.F. Bell)

22. On 23rd June 1963, the 10.05 am train had been hauled by no. 70 and after its departure nos. 62 and 50 arrive with empty stock from Fratton to form the 10.35. This will be pulled by no. 50, no. 62 taking out the next train which will be brought back by no. 70 at 11.00. (A.A.F. Bell)

24. Whilst the station was electrically lit and its through trains electrically powered, the branch line driver could, from his octogenarian steed, gaze at a mechanically operated signal, lit by oil and mounted on a pair of worn-out rails. Time passed by many branch lines and Hayling was no exception – what charm! (A.A.F. Bell)

25. A trio of weather-beaten faces – (L to R) Ron Stilwell, Dave Lear and Jock Wright. Ron has filled the scoop with chippings from his rail-mounted basket; Dave has his shovel ready to pack them under the sleeper end, whilst Jock lifts the track with a jack. The lattice structure behind Jock's head carries the up starter colour light signals. (A.A.F. Bell)

26. The arrival locomotive is still taking water at the far end of the train, whilst no. 50 had been attached ready for the next departure, on 18th August 1963. The leading coach was built in the 1930s to Maunsell's design. The unusual feature is the vertical sides to the guard/luggage area and curved sides to the passenger part. (R.C. Riley)

27. Having brought up a horse box on the front of the empty stock, no. 50 propels it back into the goods yard on the very wet morning of Sunday 1st September 1963. Near to the engine is a compartment for fodder; then come the horses' quarters, with side-hung upper doors and a lower flap which dropped onto the platform; next the groom's compartment and finally we see the opaque glass typically used on toilet compartments. (A.A.F. Bell)

28. Station staff and train crews worked two shifts and on 5th October 1963 the early turn posed before going home. The foreman was Arthur Scutt (on the left). The staff (from L to R) were Messrs. Evans (ticket collector), Cherrison (porter/ticket collector), Grout (porter), Nash (porter), Ousley (parcel clerk), Crassweller (booking clerk) and Gibbard (porter). Drivers Weeks and Hearn flank Firemen Phillips and Bradbury on the buffer beam. (A.A.F. Bell)

1963

Up	Miles	am	am	am	am	am	am		pm K	pm	pm	pm	pm	pm	pm	pm	pm		Sat am	am		am	am
Hayling Island dep	—	7 2	7 55	8 35	9 45	1055	1155	..	1255	1 55	2 58	4 16	5 6	5 57	6 47	7 52	8 52		7 2	7 55	..	8 35	9 45
North Hayling	2	7 6	7 59	8 39	9 49	1059	1159	..	1259	1 59	3 4	4 20	5 10	6 1	6 51	7 56	8 56		7 6	7 59	..	8 39	9 49
Langston	3¼	7 11	8 4	8 44	9 54	11 4	12 4	..	1 4	2 4	3 10	4 25	5 15	6 6	6 56	8 1	9 1		7 11	8 4	..	8 44	9 54
Havant arr	4½	7 15	8 8	8 48	9 58	11 8	12 8	..	1 8	2 8	3 15	4 29	5 19	6 10	7 0	8 5	9 5		7 15	8 8	..	8 48	9 58

Up	Saturdays—continued																						
	am	am	am	am		pm	pm	pm	pm	pm	pm	pm	pm		pm	pm	pm	pm	pm	pm	pm	pm	pm
Hayling Island dep	1020	1047	1120	1147	..	1220	1247	1 20	1 47	2 20	2 47	3 20	3 47	..	4 20	4 47	5 20	5 47	6 20	6 49	7 17	7 53	8 56
North Hayling	..	1051	..	1151	..	..	1251	..	1 51	..	2 51	..	3 51	..	..	4 51	..	5 51	..	6 53	7 21	7 57	9 0
Langston	..	1056	..	1156	..	..	1256	..	1 56	..	2 56	..	3 56	..	..	4 56	..	5 56	..	6 58	7 26	8 2	9 5
Havant arr	1030	11 0	1130	12 0	..	1230	1 0	1 30	2 0	2 30	3 0	3 30	4 0	..	4 30	5 0	5 30	6 0	6 30	7 2	7 30	8 6	9 9

Up	Sundays																						
	am	am	am		pm	pm	pm	pm	pm	pm	pm	pm	pm	pm		pm	pm	pm	pm	pm	pm	pm	pm
Hayling Island dep	1047	1120	1147	..	1220	1247	1 20	1 47	2 20	2 47	3 20	3 47	4 20	4 47	..	5 20	5 47	6 20	6 47	7 20	7 47	8 20	8 36
North Hayling	1051	..	1151	..	1251	..	1 51	..	2 51	..	3 51	..	4 51	..	..	5 51	..	6 51	..	7 51	8 24		
Langston	1056	..	1156	..	1256	..	1 56	..	2 56	..	3 56	..	4 56	..	..	5 56	..	6 56	..	7 56	8 29		
Havant arr	11 0	1130	12 0	..	1230	1 0	1 30	2 0	2 30	3 0	3 30	4 0	4 30	5 0	..	5 30	6 0	6 30	7 0	7 30	8 0	8 33	8 46

K Commences 8th July

29. Before starting late turn on the same day, the staff and train crew posed in front of no. 46. The Stationmaster, Mr. E.G.H. Clarke, joined the group with Driver Chick, Porters Budd, Clarke and Baldwin, with Foreman Les Horwood holding the staff. Porters Bryden and Ware with Booking Clerk Willmott completed the line-up. The fireman's name has not survived the passage of time. We can also see the detail of the spark arrester – very few BR locomotives were so fitted. (A.A.F. Bell)

1924

HAVANT and HAYLING ISLAND.—Southern.

Down.	Week Days.																Sundays.					
	mrn	mrn	mrn	mrn	mrn	aft	aft	E	S	aft	E	S	aft	aft	aft	aft	mrn	mrn	mrn	aft	aft	aft	aft
Havant ....dep.	7 0	7 39	8 32	9 20	10 28	12 8	1 5	1 55	2 7	3 3	4 30	4 35	5 42	6 50	7 38	8 23	9 15	9	9 10	0	11 45	2 30	4 0 6 30 7 45
Langston	...	7 43	8 36	9 24	10 32	12 12		9 1	59	2 11	3 7	4 34	4 39	5 46	6 54	7 42	8 27	9 22	9	13	10	4	11 49	2 34	4 4 6 34 7 49
North Hayling	...	7 49	8 42	9 30	10 38	12 18	1 52		6	2 17	3 13	4 40	4 45	5 52	7 0	7 48	8 33	9 24	9	19	10	10	11 55	2 40	4 10 6 40 7 55
Hayling Island ....arr.	7 10	7 54	8 47	9 35	10 43	12 23	1 20	2 10	2 22	3 18	4 45	4 50	5 57	7 5	7 52	8 38	9 33	9 24	10	15	12 0	2 45	4 15 6 45 8 0

Up.	Week Days.																Sundays.					
	mrn	mrn	mrn	mrn	mrn	aft	aft	aft	aft	aft	aft	aft	aft	aft	aft	mrn	mrn	aft	aft	aft	aft	aft	aft
Hayling Island ....dep.	7 17	8	1	8 54	10 5	10 50	12 35	1	2 7	2 40	3 25	4 58	6	5 7	13	8	0 8	45	9 42	9	32	10 40	2 0	3 15 5 5 7 0 8 30
North Hayling	7 22	8		6	8 59	....	10 55	12 40	1	3 2	2 45	3 30	5	3 6	10	7	18	8	5	8 50	9 47	9	37	10 45	2 5	3 20 6	0 7	5 8 35
Langston......213, 216	7 28	8	12	9	5	....	11 1	12 46	1	38	2 51	3 36	5	9	6 16	7	24	8 11	8 56	9 53	9	43	10 51	2 11	3 26 6	6 7 11 8 41
Havant 179, 210, arr.	7 32	8	16	9	9	10 15	11 5	12 51	1	42	2 55	3 40	5	13	6 20	7 28	8 15	9	0	9 57	9	47	10 55	2 15	3 30 6	10 7 15 8 45

30. On the last day of passenger services, no. 50 takes water at the end of the line. This was the only water supply on the branch. The box on the right, bearing a black cross, con-tained a telephone. From here the signalman was advised when to move the loop points so that the engine could run round its train. (R.C. Riley)

32. Looking west along the 80-lever frame in the presence of Signalman Harry Griffin and Signal Lad Michael Prior. The latter is working on the train register, a book in which every train movement is recorded. Note the stand-by oil lamps. Tyers Block Instrument for the safe working of the single line branch is seen at the end of the block shelf behind the signalman's head. (A.A.F. Bell)

31. Looking north along New Lane, we see the former gasworks building beyond the wide gates of the main line crossing. Their plain concrete posts are drab compared with the octagonal cast iron posts of the branch crossing. Although the road was narrow, double gates were provided. The signal box also controlled the branch and was known as East Box until 1938, when it was extended to take over the functions of the two redundant boxes. Wheels were provided to control both sets of level crossing gates and a lever locked the wicket gates in the foreground. (A.A.F. Bell)

33. The driver leans out well to collect the staff for single line working being held up by the signalman on 15th August 1954. Normally the staff was retained on the engine when only one train was running on the branch but the rules had been tightened up by then and it had to be handed in and collected on each trip. (A.A.F. Bell)

35. Signal & Telegraph Lineman Ted Good-land and his mate Harry Tannandine were responsible for the whole branch. Here they are seen checking the electrical locking on the turn out leading to the main line. Note the fine ornate capping to the Saxby & Farmer gate post. (A.A.F. Bell)

Table 37   HAVANT and HAYLING ISLAND

Miles	Down							Week Days													
		a.m	a.m	a.m	a.m	a.m	a.m	p.m	p.m	p.m	p.m	p.m	p.m	SX	SO	SX	SO	SX	SO
	Havant............dep	6 35	7 34	8 20	9 12	10 19	11 19	12 36	1 34	2 27	3 34	4 42	5 33	6 20	6 34	7 20	7 34	8 20	8 34
1	Langston................	6 38	7 37	8 23	9 15	10 22	11 22	12 39	1 37	2 23	3 37	4 45	5 36	6 23	6 37	7 23	7 37	8 23	8 37
2¼	North Hayling..........	..	7 41	8 27	9 22	10 26	11 26	12 43	1 41	2 27	3 41	4 49	5 40	6 27	6 41	7 27	7 41	8 27	8 41
4¼	Hayling Island.......arr	6 48	7 47	8 33	9 28	10 32	11 32	12 49	1 47	2 33	3 47	4 55	5 46	6 33	6 47	7 33	7 47	8 33	8 47

Miles	Up							Week Days										
		a.m	a.m	a.m	a.m	a.m	a.m	p.m	p.m	SX	SO	p.m	p.m	p.m	SX	SO	p.m	p.m
	Hayling Island.......dep	7 7	8 08	8 40	9 45	10 52	11 55	1255	1 55	2 53	2 57	4 16	5 6	5 57	6 50	6 52	7 52	8 52
2	North Hayling..........	7 11	8 48	8 44	9 49	10 56	11 59	1259	1 59	2 59	3 1	4 20	5 10	6 1	6 54	6 56	7 56	8 56
3¼	Langston................	7 16	8 9	8 49	9 54	11 1	12 4	1 4	2 4	3 5	3 6	4 25	5 15	6 6	6 59	7 1	8 1	9 1
4¼	Havant.................arr	7 20	8 15	8 53	9 58	11 5	12 8	1 8	2 8	3 10	3 10	4 29	5 19	6 10	7 3	7 5	8 5	9 5

Down			Sundays					
			Commencing 1st May, 1955					
		a.m	a.m	p.m	p.m	p.m	p.m	p.m
Havant............dep	10 35	11 35	12 35	1 35	2 35	3 35	5 35,6 35,6 35	7 35
Langston................	10 38	11 38	12 38	1 38	2 38	3 38	5 38,6 38,7 38	
North Hayling..........	10 42	11 42	12 42	1 42	2 42	3 42	5 42,6 42,7 42	
Hayling Island.......arr	10 48	11 48	12 48	1 48	2 48	3 48	5 48,6 48,7 48	

Up			Sundays					
			Commencing 1st May, 1955					
		a.m	a.m	p.m	p.m	p.m	p.m	p.m
Hayling Island.......dep	10 55	11 55	12 55	1 55	2 55	4 55	5 55,6 55,7 55	..
North Hayling..........	10 59	11 59	12 59	1 59	2 59	4 59	5 59,6 59,7 59	..
Langston................	11 4	12 4	1 4	2 4	3 4	5 4	6 4, 7 4, 8 4	..
Havant.................arr	11 8	12 8	1 8	2 8	3 8	5 8	6 8, 7 8, 8 8	..

SO Saturdays only.   SX Saturdays excepted

1955

34. The gates had to be closed each time a locomotive ran round its train. This is the signalman's view of no. 78 performing that duty. Behind her is the former Labour Exchange and an old-style SCHOOL road sign. The short length of road between the crossings was repaired by BR, who continued to have that responsibility for many years after the branch had closed and the track lifted. (A.A.F. Bell)

36. We saw in picture no. 22 nos. 62 and 50 arriving with empty stock. This view was taken about four minutes later, after no. 62 had been uncoupled. No. 50 then propelled its train back into the bay; uncoupled; ran round the train; took water; ran round again and waited whilst no. 62 ran into the loop. No. 50 departed as the 10.35 and no. 62 took water before leaving with the 11.05.
(A.A.F. Bell)

37. Rounding the sharp curve (only 8 chains radius) is no. 36, one of the oldest Terriers still in use in September 1963, hauling one of the most modern coaches. The one with a light colour roof is no. S1000S, the only one ever to be built of glass reinforced plastic. It is now preserved on the East Somerset Railway. The ground signal was the one used to call on no. 62 in the previous picture.
(A.A.F. Bell)

38. A typical Southern Railway branch train in 1938 with a guards compartment at each end. This Terrier was built in 1877, carried the name *Fulham* for sometime and was withdrawn in 1951. It is about to pass under the bridge carrying East Street, which was part of the A27 at that time. The gasworks chimney stack can be seen in the distance. (C.R.L. Coles)

39. This is the same location as the previous picture but 23 years later. No. 40 hauls four coaches and an ex-GWR Fruit D van as the shadows lengthen on a fine June evening. (R.S. Greenwood)

40. Looking south under the East Street bridge at the only other over bridge on the line – a steel lattice footbridge. An afternoon up train enters the reverse curves of Town Hall cutting in August 1960. (A.A.F. Bell)

41. A fine view of a Hayling-bound train in 1939, seen from Wade Court crossing (see introductory map). The stream alongside the railway was so pure that watercress beds were established close to the line for many years. This Terrier was built in 1878 and in 1946 it became the Brighton Locomotive Works shunter. It replaced the better known no. 82 *Boxhill*, now in the National Railway Museum, and was similarly repainted in the original livery chosen by their designer, Mr. William Stroudley. (C.R.L. Coles)

42. The 11.35 from Havant on 19th July 1959 required additional accommodation for holiday-makers' luggage and perambulators. It was not unusual for a "Pram Van" to be attached to passenger trains in the last summers of the line. (L. Elsey)

LANGSTON

43. Soon after taking over the operation of the line the LBSCR dropped the 'e' from Langstone although it continues to be used elsewhere to this day. The small signal cabin appears to be the one still in use at the time of closure. The two parts of the station building appear to have been erected at different times as the roofs and board positions are different. Although re-roofed and re-boarded, it too seems to have lasted to the end. The low wooden platform however was replaced in 1949-50 by a pre-cast concrete structure originally sent to North Hayling but not erected there. Two points of interest are the poor ballasting and lack of proper shoulders. No doubt these were some of the economy features that caused displeasure to the Inspecting Officer.
(D.G. Dine collection)

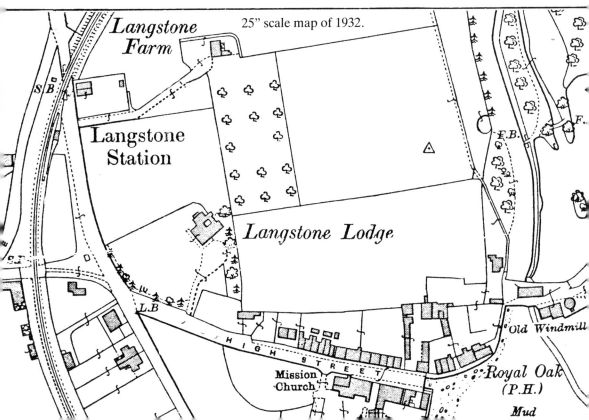

44. No. 78 *Knowle* was one of the first Terriers to work on the branch and its varied career is described at the beginning of this album. The four-wheeled coaches no doubt gave passengers a rough ride. Notice that the rear brake van has passenger compartments, the front one has an oil lamp housing on the roof and one signal wire has sagged.
(O.J. Morris/Lens of Sutton)

45. Photographed at 5.46 pm on 3rd October 1925, no. 653 (formerly no. 53 *Ashstead*) had not yet been repainted in Southern Railway livery. In 1937 it was sold to the independent Weston, Clevedon and Portishead Railway in Somerset, another Col. Stephen's line.
(O.J. Morris/Lens of Sutton)

46. The details of this vintage transport scene were not recorded. The LBSCR gates can be compared with later photographs of the SR pattern which had cross bracing and split discs.
(N. Shepherd/R.C. Riley collection)

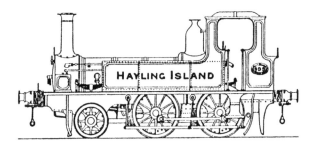

→

48. The delayed motorist's view. No. 46, in profile, waiting to depart for Havant on 25th June 1961. (E. Wilmshurst)

47. Originally no. 62 *Martello*, this Terrier was another which spent many years working the branch and was subsequently preserved. After withdrawal in 1963 it became an exhibit at Butlins Holiday Camp, Ayr, and is now at the Bressingham Steam Museum near Diss.
(O.J. Morris/E.R. Lacey collection)

49. Two railway men were required on Summer Saturdays to wage war against the dense road traffic. Some modern concrete products are evident – lamp posts, sleepers, fence posts and platform decking. Evidence of the past is also to be seen – the LBSCR station name board with raised metal lettering, still in use 40 years after the company ceased to exist. The bus is a 1948 54-seater Leyland PD2/1, withdrawn in 1965. A short life when compared with the Terrier that is delaying it. (A.A.F. Bell)

→

51. The view from the booking office window gives another opportunity to appreciate the disparity in height and width of the Terriers in relation to the passenger coaches. (A.A.F. Bell)

50. The six-lever ground frame was not the original but was an ex-LSWR Mackenzie & Holland product. Albert Grout was operating it on 9th June 1963, whilst the crossing keeper, Jack Dalton, waited to open the heavy gates by hand. The weather-boarded cottage stands today as a convenient way of locating the former site of the crossing. (A.A.F. Bell)

52. On 14th September 1963 Driver Fellows (on the right) was making his final trip on the branch. On the platform is Crossing Keeper O'Shea (wearing his taxi driver's hat) with Relief Keeper Prior. The leading coach had end windows fitted for push-pull working but was not used in this manner on the branch. (A.A.F. Bell)

54. The lamp changer's view of part of one of the massive traffic jams created by the original engineer's failure to provide a bridge as planned. Until 1960 motorists were further frustrated by delays at the toll bridge. No. 46 is seen here starting a northbound train on 28th September 1963. (A.A.F. Bell)

←

53. The waiting room doubled up as booking hall and ladder store. Nature contrived invariably to produce a draught through the aperture at the booking office grille which drew bank notes from passengers' fingers onto the counter below. On the wall is the timetable poster so valuable to the true traveller and so infuriating to passengers only wishing to go to the next station. (A.A.F. Bell)

55. A single lattice post served to support the Langston Crossing Up Home and the Langston Bridge Fixed Distant signals. No. 70 is on an up train on 27th April 1963. (A.A.F. Bell)

SOUTHERN RAILWAY.
Issued subject to the Bye-laws, Regulations & Conditions in the Company's Bills and Notices.

Havant to

Havant
Langston

Havant
Langston

LANGSTON

THIRD CLASS

THIRD CLASS

Fare 3d

Fare 8d

NOT TRANSFERABLE

4035   4035

2nd - SINGLE

SINGLE - 2nd

Hayling Island to

Hayling Island
Langston

Hayling Island
Langston

LANGSTON

(S)

1/- Fare 1/-

(S)

For conditions see over   For conditions see over

6938   6938

56. Mixed trains (i.e. passengers and goods) were permitted by the Board of Trade on certain trains on a number of branches. This is the 9.20 am ex-Havant on 29th July 1931 passing the end of the former wharf siding head shunt. Loose coupled wagons had to be placed behind the passenger coaches. (O.J. Morris/E.R. Lacey collection)

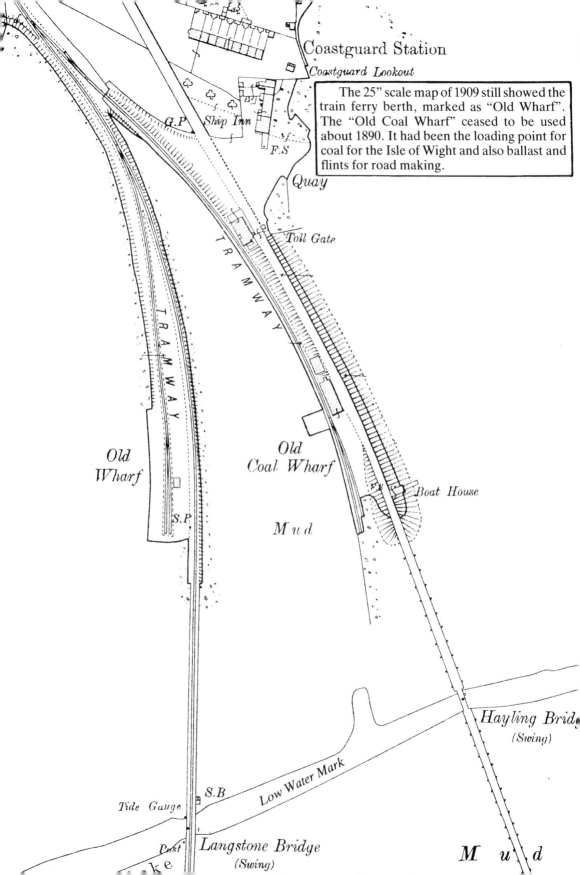

Coastguard Station

Coastguard Lookout

The 25" scale map of 1909 still showed the train ferry berth, marked as "Old Wharf". The "Old Coal Wharf" ceased to be used about 1890. It had been the loading point for coal for the Isle of Wight and also ballast and flints for road making.

G.P

Ship Inn

F.S

Quay

Toll Gate

T R A M W A Y

T R A M W A Y

Old
Wharf

Old
Coal Wharf

Boat House

F.S

S.P.

M u d

Hayling Brid
(Swing)

Low Water Mark

Tide Gauge

S.B

Post

Langstone Bridge
(Swing)

M u d

The ISLE of WIGHT
MARINE TRANSIT COMPANY

The Langston-Brading Train Ferry was the first train ferry to operate in the South of England and the only one ever to run to the Isle of Wight. It also had the distinction of operating the only vessel that the North British Railway sold out of service from their Firth of Forth and Firth of Tay fleets. The method by which the wagons were loaded and unloaded were unique.

The difference between high water and low water could be as much as 20ft, and means to find a way to transport wagons across the Firth were in the minds of various people. Thomas Bouch, the Engineer and Manager of the Edinburgh and Northern Railway was mainly responsible for the design of what The Illustrated London News of February 16th 1850 called a "Floating Railroad". The first vessel, the *Leviathan* ran between Granton and Burntisland on the Forth, and the service, with various different steamers, lasted until the Forth Rail Bridge was opened in 1890.

The success of this service prompted the opening of a similar service across the Tay, and this ran from Tayport to Broughty Ferry. The first vessel built for this route was the *Carrier*, launched on 16th November 1858. In 1878 when the Tay Bridge was opened, the *Carrier* was transferred to the Forth as a spare vessel. Thomas Bouch's design for the Tay Bridge was, as history has so well recorded, by no means as practical as his Train Ferries, and following the fall of the bridge in 1879, the *Carrier* was reinstated and continued to cross the Tay until withdrawn and sold in 1882.

At this point the history of the Isle of

---

57. The *P.S. Carrier* was photographed at Burntisland with the *P.S. John Stirling* in the background. It steamed south in 1882 to Newhaven Harbour where some repairs were undertaken at the LBSCR marine workshops. It was built by Scott & Co. of Greenock in 1858 and weighed 243 tons. There were two cylinders of a mere 36" stroke operating a single crankshaft which was cheaper than the normal arrangement of independent paddle wheels. Curved plates covering the cranks can be seen between the pairs of rails. Wagons were winched on and off the vessel with a rope from a stationary steam winding engine on the shore.
(British Rail/C.E.C Townsend collection)

58. As no picture is available of the bow end of the *P.S. Carrier* we included a photograph of a loaded model, made by Alan Bell. The paddle wheels were unusually small for a vessel 124 ft long. In 1887 the LBSCR attempted to reduce its losses on the vessel's operation by carrying passengers on a review of the Naval Fleet. It apparently sailed ahead of the Royal Yacht, belching black smoke. Queen Victoria was not amused. An enlargement of the ticket is reproduced here and shows the unofficial spelling. (A.A.F. Bell)

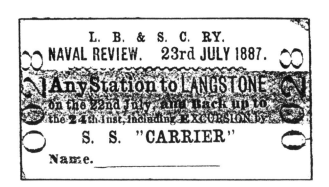

L. B. & S. C. RY.
NAVAL REVIEW. 23rd JULY 1887.
Any Station to LANGSTONE
on the 22nd July, and back up to
the 24th inst, including EXCURSION by
S. S. "CARRIER"
Name.

Wight Marine Transit Company begins with the sale of the *Carrier*, together with the moveable cradles, and the winding engines from Tayport and Broughty Ferry to Samuel Lack Mason, a Director of the North British Railway Company and also of the new company. Agreements were drawn up between the IOWMTCo and the London Brighton and South Coast Railway Company, regarding the traffic between the mainland and the Isle of Wight, it being part of the contract that the Portsmouth-Ryde and Langston-Brading routes were not in competition with each other so far as goods traffic was concerned.

The sale price is reported as being £3 400, which seems a small amount these days, but all the equipment (vessel included) was over 20 years old at time of sale.

A specification for the ramps at Langston and at St. Helens Quay in Brading Harbour indicated that the ramps, winding gear and engines were awaiting transportation from Newhaven in 1883, and a Prospectus dated 12th March 1884 set out the details of the new scheme. The Capital was £30,000 in 3000 shares of £10 each, and the cost to the company of Works at Langston and Brading was limited to £28 425.

Unfortunately, after a year of operation,

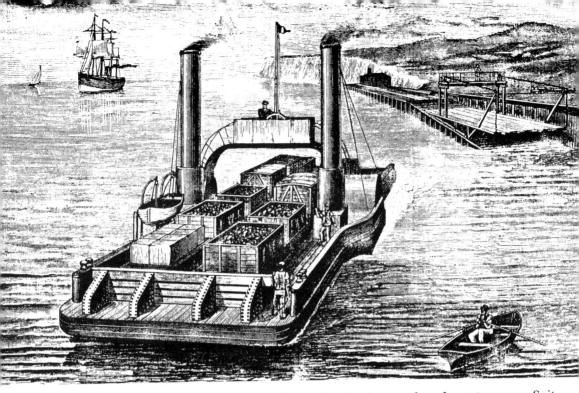

the finances of the Marine Transport Co. were such that the LB&SCR made an Agreement with the Company, dated 23rd December 1885, for the hire of the *Carrier* and the use of the quays at each end of the route.

The service was continued until 1888 and apparently the uncertain weather had much to do with the erratic running of the vessel, which had been designed, as we have seen, to cross the more enclosed waters of the Firth of Tay. The journey from Langston across Spithead to Brading Harbour was 11 miles, of which 4½ were in the two harbours, and 6½ miles in the open sea, where frequent rough weather (familiar to many regular commuters between Portsmouth and Ryde) made the service uncertain and expensive.

The last recorded trip by the *Carrier* was in March of that year but later trips could have been made.

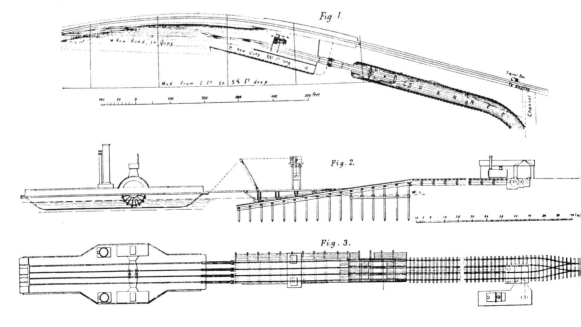

Fig 1.

Fig. 2.

Fig. 3.

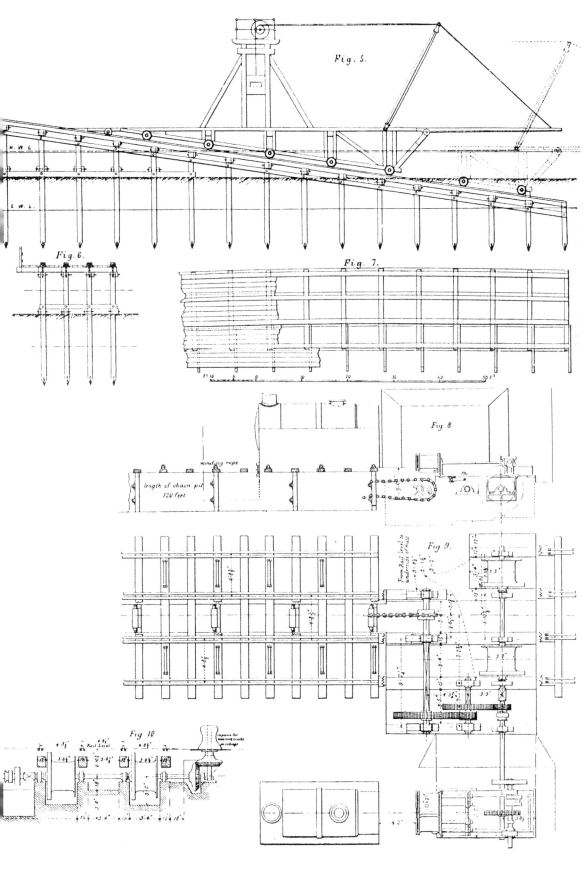

Fig. 5.

H. W. L.

L. W. L.

Fig. 6.

Fig. 7.

Fig 8

winding rope

length of chain pit
120 feet

Fig 9.

From Rail Level to
underside of rail

Fig 10

Rail Level

Capstan for
empty trucks
at sidings

The following report, dated 7th August 1885, is reproduced from *Engineering*, by kind permission of the Editor. The background to the engraving was intended to represent the Isle of Wight.

THE ISLE OF WIGHT STEAM FERRY.

THE works at Langston Harbour, near Portsmouth, and at Brading, in the Isle of Wight, designed to effect the transport of trains of railway vehicles bodily across the Solent, were completed on Wednesday last, and on Thursday the appliances which have more than once been used provisionally during the execution of the works, were pronounced ready for regular traffic. We give drawings of the full details, on pages 126 and 127, and it should be stated that no claim is laid to mechanical novelty—their merit lies in the ingenuity in which commonplace mechanical arrangements have been applied to achieve in a simple way an exceedingly useful purpose. Railways existing on the mainland and in the Isle of Wight, with their lines coming down to the seaside, the problem to be solved was how to transfer simply, cheaply, and expeditiously from the railways to the deck of seagoing vessels, railway vehicles without disturbance of their load. Once upon the deck of the steamer, supposing only she be adapted to the carrying of a heavy deck load, the transport is simple enough—the thing is the loading and unloading, and to be useful this must be accomplished by means more expeditious and less costly than the ordinary method of handling and transhipment. The distance to be traversed between Brading and Langston is between 10 and 11 miles, 6½ miles are in the open sea, the rest in landlocked harbours, which on the island as on the mainland have been judiciously chosen as the places of arrival and departure. On both sides the process of loading and unloading goes on in perfectly still water, and on both the mechanical arrangements are the same. The amount of structural work on the island was rather less than that necessary on the mainland, owing to somewhat less favourable conditions at Langston. It goes without saying that on both sides there is direct physical connection with the railway systems. At Brading all the railways in the island are communicated with, while at Langston access is obtained to the Hayling Island branch of the Brighton and South Coast Railway, which at Havant has a junction with the London and South-Western system—to London by the direct Portsmouth line as well as to Southampton and the west of England.

At Langston the railway skirts the sea. Alongside of, and parallel to, the railway and upon the foreshore, an embankment has been built about 700 yards in length, and of width varying from 30 to 40 yards. The side or sea face of this embankment is sloped and pitched in the customary manner for its entire length, save 300 ft. at the extremity, where a wharf is formed suitable to the use for loading and discharging of ordinary seagoing craft. From the end of the embankment a sloped timber jetty projects, commencing at the rail level and descending by a gradient of 1 in 8, to 4 ft. below the natural bed of the sea. From the top to the bottom of this slope are laid eight ordinary permanent way rails, four of which constitute two running lines of the standard gauge, and along which, as presently explained, the railway vehicles pass, and four laid close, and parallel, to each of the running rails. These latter act as check rails, but fulfil also a more important purpose to be described.

In carrying the wagons on board the steamer they are placed upon two lines running from stem to stern. In discharging and loading them, the vessel approaches the sloping jetty stern on, bringing the parallel rails upon her deck into line with the rails laid upon the sloping jetty. It follows that when the tide is high and covers the greater part of the slope, the level of the steamer's deck approaches the level of the top of the jetty; when the tide is low, the steamer approaches at a lower level and a considerable part of the slope is exposed; but neither at high or low tide can the stern of the steamer be brought sufficiently near to the fixed slope to admit of wagons passing from the one to the other. There is always a hiatus which must be bridged. The four extra rails above mentioned are useful in this connection. They carry the moving bridge or cradle, which passing up and down the sloping jetty in the varying states of the tide, connect the ship, at whatever height her deck, with the rails on shore.

In Fig. 2 of our drawings the cradle is shown in position for loading the steamer at low water. In Fig. 5 it is shown on a larger scale as at medium tide; the dotted fragment of the drawing indicating the position at dead low water. The cradle, which is supported on 20 wheels, resting five on each of the four rails of the jetty, is of timber with wrought iron attachments and cast-iron wheels, the movable drawbridge being balanced so as to be well within the power of a single man. It is moved up and down the slope by means of drawing engines, Fig. 9, which also drive two horizontal drums 3 ft. in diameter, by means of which wagons are lowered on to and drawn up from the deck of the steamer. The drawing engines are a pair of ordinary winding engines of 60 horse-power. Attached to the drawing machinery is a movable shunting capstan for economising locomotive power in the station yard. The steamer shown in the perspective view, and in Figs. 2 and 3, is of iron and of great strength, her dimensions being: Length 130 ft., breadth of beam 26 ft., horse-power 150 nominal, draught loaded 5 ft. 9 in. She has the steam steering gear of the Harrison type.

The deck arrangement is noteworthy, from the position of the lines of rails. What would in an ordinary railway be the 6 ft. space, is 4 ft. 8½ in. It follows, therefore, that in the event of there not being a sufficient number of wagons to occupy the two outer lines of rails, the load may be placed amidships on the centre line, and so contribute to the steadiness and trim of the vessel at sea. The process of loading and discharging may be briefly described. On the approach of the ship, with her cargo aboard, the person ashore in charge of the engines and cradle observes the state of the tide, and, knowing the draught of water, adjusts the cradle by lowering it or raising it to the required level. On the vessel coming into position, the drawbridge, which is raised and depressed by crabs worked from the gantry, is lowered on to the steamer's prow and made fast there. Ropes, which are ready on the drawbridge connected with the winding gear, are then hooked on to the coupling chains of the foremost wagons, and on signal being given the whole train is drawn out at one operation. The time occupied in unloading is regulated by the speed at which the engines are run, and this may be fast or slow according to the condition of the tide and other circumstances. At high tide, when the deck of the steamer and the cradle are nearly level with the rails at the top of the slope, the process of discharging may last some 30 or 40 seconds. At dead low water, when the slope is at its maximum of steepness, a slower speed is advisable, and the time occupied may vary from 2 to 4 minutes. The loading, which is accomplished on a similar principle, requires rather more caution. The wagons being drawn to the verge of the slope by steam shunting gear attached to the winding engines, are then allowed to run on to the deck by their own gravity, checked and regulated by the ropes attached to the drums.

When the project was first mooted, doubts were freely expressed as to the sufficiency of traffic to warrant an establishment of this kind. Recently, however, doubts on this subject have been resolved, and it is now anticipated that difficulty is more likely to arise from redundancy than deficiency of freight. The present carrying power, judging from the traffic that is already offering, is likely to require augmentation. Already inland coal traffic is tendered for conveyance fully up to the carrying power, and other branches of traffic to which the system lends itself if presented in the quantity that seems probable, can only be accommodated by an additional vessel. As some indication of the need for improvement which the Transit Company supplies, we quote from an official source a brief description of the plan which the new arrangements supersede. Speaking of goods seeking delivery at the Isle of Wight the writer remarks :

"At Portsmouth, where the first handling and delay occurs, everything must be unloaded at the town station and take turn with Portsmouth town goods ; then follows cartage through the town to the quay, and two more handlings occur here in unloading the carts and shipping.

"Arrived at Ryde the goods are moved again for cartage to the station (through the town of Ryde), and once more there in loading into railway wagons.

"At Ventnor, or other destination, the reverse process occurs, and after two more handlings and another cartage, the consignee is at last reached, and it is well if he has nothing to complain of in the condition of his goods.

"Since arriving at Portsmouth there have been seven separate handlings, three cartages, a risky water passage, and a railway journey. Although the railway company's responsibility continued throughout, their actual control ceased at Portsmouth, when possession was transferred to the Isle of Wight agents or carriers."

In the future, by contrast, vehicles loaded in London will go direct to their railway destination with no more disturbance to bulk or change of vehicle than is involved in a railway journey between London and Birmingham. The whole of the costly and cumbersome terminal services at Portsmouth and Ryde will be avoided.

The plans and local installations are from the design of Mr. Samuel L. Mason, of Edinburgh, who was also the originator of the scheme. He has closely followed the arrangements of the North British Company at Burntisland, of which he had experience when formerly general manager of that company. The work has been financed and constructed by him, the resident engineer being Mr. William Gregory, C.E. Mr. Stroudley, C.E., of the London, Brighton, and South Coast Railway Locomotive Department, constructed and erected the machinery.

It is in great measure due to the enterprise of the Brighton Board, to their manager, Mr. J. P. Knight, goods manager Mr. Stainforth, and to Mr. Spencer Balfour, M.P., that the Isle of Wight is secured the possession of an economic means of communication of great promise and capability. The Brighton Company have, we are informed, entered into agreements by which they adopt the new route for the whole of their traffic, under conditions which give assurances of financial success.

ISLE OF WIGHT MARINE TRANSIT COMPANY LIMITED

59. An up train passing by the site of the former train ferry berth on 21st March 1936. On the extreme left is the road bridge and the piles of the old coal wharf. Note the goods guards van being returned to Havant following its use on a down mixed train (H.C. Casserley)

1878 Excursion Handbill

London Brighton and South Coast Railway
(THE DIRECT MID-SUSSEX ROUTE.)

CHEAP DAY EXCURSION
TO
HAYLING ISLAND
EVERY WEDNESDAY.

From **LONDON BRIDGE** 6.50 a.m.

From **VICTORIA** ... ... 6.40 a.m,

Calling at CLAPHAM JUNCTION 6.45 a.m.

RETURNING from South Hayling 7.0 p.m.

FARES THERE AND BACK:

First Class.	Second Class.	Third Class.
11/-	**7/6**	**5/-**

Children under Twelve Years of age, Half-price.

Passengers with Luggage charged Ordinary Fares. Tickets not Transferable; only available by the above Train, and on the date of issue.

The Victoria Tickets are available to return to London Bridge, and *vice versâ.*

London Bridge, June, 1878.   (By Order) **J. P. KNIGHT,** *General Manager.*

(10,000(—34-5-78.)   Waterlow and Sons Limited Printers, London Wall, London.

60. During World War II, heavy armaments arriving by road had to be dismantled at this point and transferred to railway wagons, owing to the severe weight limits of the road bridge. To facilitate this an extra siding with the end loading dock (seen on the left) was provided – but not until six years after the war had ended! The sidings were used only by railway engineers. The concrete blocks on the right are protecting the bank from erosion by the sea and were parts of "pill boxes" and gun emplacements. (S.C. Nash)

61. This well known photographer has endorsed his work so we say no more. (E.R. Lacey collection)

B655 on 9.30am Harbour-Hayling Mixed 25/5/32 by H.Morris

Copyright H.Morris

62. No. 46 approaching the 20 mph speed restriction sign for the bridge, the 1½ mile post and the gradient post. The smoke was generated for the benefit of the photographer, six weeks before the line's closure. (A.A.F. Bell)

63. The 2.58 pm from Hayling was the mixed train in latter years and is seen here on the 14th October 1963, hauled by no. 46. The archaeology of the *Carrier* berth in the foreground can still be seen today. The electricity pylon was erected in 1946 in mid-channel and carries the conductors between the wooden poles on the shores. (A.A.F. Bell)

64. Another view of the same train and the sea defences at this normally peaceful location. However, back in 1866 a storm of such ferocity raged that more than 300 trees were uprooted in the area. (A.A.F. Bell)

65. No. 32636 (originally no. *72 Fenchurch*) was chosen to haul the last train as it was the oldest working locomotive on BR. This was run on Sunday 3rd November 1963, the day after the last public train had run. (No. 70 was at the rear of the train). The level grass in the foreground had been the site of the Coal Wharf. (S.C. Nash)

LANGSTON BRIDGE

66. An original London Brighton and South Coast Railway Postcard numbered Series 4. On the reverse is printed "Langston Harbour Swing Bridge carries the Hayling Island Branch single line over the Harbour about 1½ miles south of Havant, thus connecting this charming little Island with the Main Land. The opening over the water-way has a span of 30 feet for the passage of vessels. The girders of the opening portion are pivoted on a wrought iron cyclinder and travel round a roller path, the wheel gearing being worked by hand." The boat is probably *Langstone*, owned by Littles of Langstone and used mainly for the transportation of gravel. (E. Jackson collection)

67. The railway-owned road bridge caused great distress to bus passengers when the weight restriction was further reduced to a mere five tons in 1954. As already recounted, many passengers were forced to walk over the bridge whilst their partly loaded bus went ahead of them. After protests were made, a Leyland Cub was provided to operate a shuttle service over the bridge. Its seats were arranged longitudinally (as in World War II *Standee* buses) and to reduce its weight further, the rear indicator box and inside wheels were removed! Just visible, is the embankment of the new bridge on the left and old bridge toll keeper's hut on the right. (A.A.F. Bell)

SOUTHERN RAILWAY

LIST OF TOLLS

To be paid on passing over Hayling Bridge.

	Each way	
	s.	d.
For every person on foot, and if with a wheelbarrow or such like carriage, the sum of		½
For every horse, mule or ass		2
For every horse, mule or ass carrying double		3
For every bull, ox, cow, steer or heifer or calf		1
For every sheep, lamb, boar, sow or pig		1
If a score or more, then at the rate per score		10
For every hearse, with or without a corpse (drawn by one or two horses)	2	0
If drawn by three or more horses	2	6
For every coach, chariot, chaise, berlin landau, phaeton or other carriage on springs, with four or three wheels and drawn by four horses or other beast of draught	1	6
If drawn by three horses or other beast of draught	1	3
If drawn by two horses or other beast of draught		9
If drawn by one horse or other beast of draught		6
For every gig, whiskey, chair or other carriage hung on springs with two wheels drawn by not more than two horses or other beast of draught		8
If drawn by one horse or other beast of draught		4
For every wagon, timber carriage, wain, dray, truck or such like carriage drawn by six or more horses or other beast of draught	1	6
If drawn by five horses or other beast of draught	1	3
If drawn by four horses or other beast of draught	1	0
If drawn by three horses or other beast of draught		10
If drawn by two horses or other beast of draught		9
For every cart drawn by four horses or other beast of draught	1	3
If drawn by three horses or other beast of draught	1	0
If drawn by two horses or other beast of draught		8
If drawn by one horse or other beast of draught		4
For every traction engine weighing two tons or less		6
If over two tons but not exceeding four tons		9
If over four tons		10
For every trailer drawn by a traction engine or by a motor or steam lorry in addition to the charge for the traction engine or motor steam lorry		3
For every motor or steam lorry or commercial motor vehicle weighing two tons or less		6
If over two tons but not exceeding four tons		9
If over four tons		10
For every private motor car		4
For every private motor car—for passing and repassing—return		8
For every motor car (other than a private motor car) and for every char-a-banc or other such vehicle used for conveying passengers if weighing two tons or less		9
If weighing over two tons but not exceeding four tons	1	0
If weighing over four tons	1	6
For every cycle not constructed to be propelled by mechanical power		½
For every motor cycle		2
For every fore carriage, side carriage, trailer or vehicle attached to any cycle		1

C.X. 5/³⁰⁄₁₂ ₄₄ ¹⁰⁰   December, 1944.

E. J. MISSENDEN,
General Manager.

68. The following sequence of photographs of the bridge were all taken in 1963 to create a full record of this interesting historic structure. First, two for the price of one – a full reflection of the trestles in the calm waters of an August morning, as the first train of the day rumbles across to the Island. In the foreground is the old road. (A.A.F. Bell)

69. The opening of the bridge became less frequent, for example, in 1949 it was only opened nine times. Here no. 50 with an up train is about to pass the post used for raising the signals to water borne traffic. Note the signal wire that had to be disconnected by the signalman before the bridge was opened. (J. Scrace)

70. The signal box ceased to be manned full time about 1938. Anyone wishing to have the bridge opened had to notify Havant station and agree a mutually convenient time for the operation. Only four of the seven levers were in use. Few passengers would have realised that the southern end of the bridge was so curved. (A.A.F. Bell)

71. Definitely fishermen and not railway enthusiasts. Their fraternity were often seen illegally practising their sport from the bridge. The hut contained fire buckets for use on the timber decking after the passage of engines with defective ashpans.
(A.A.F. Bell)

73. Here we see the other pair of fishplate that had to be removed, together with th locking bolts operated from the signal bo which were interlocked with the signals. Th circular walk way can also be seen. The tw men would engage cranked poles, each abo six feet long, into the pinion shaft and simp keep walking! (R.C. Riley)

72. The D-shaped objects are weights used for counter balancing the cantilevered part of the swinging span. A lengthman was required to remove the fishplates in the foreground and he would then assist the signalman in swinging the bridge. Notice also the removable link in the signal wire. (A.A.F. Bell)

74. The small pinion gear is visible under the centre of the decking. Notice also the circular balcony for the maintenance engineers. A similar projection was provided to enable the signalman to escape from the open span to operate the shipping signal. (A.A.F. Bell)

75. By May of 1964 vandals had amazingly removed the swing span counterweights, rendering the bridge immobile. As a result we see a yachtsman and his lady resorting to taking their vessel through on its side, whilst swimming to achieve propulsion.
(A.A.F. Bell)

In 1930 the following notice was issued to mariners – "On a vessel approaching the railway bridge, the bridge-man will hoist on the flagstaff at the centre of the bridge a white flag by day, or a white light by night, to denote that the vessel is seen. If the bridge can be safely opened, a black ball will be hoisted by day and a green light by night. When the bridge is actually open, a red flag will be hoisted by day and red light by night, and shown until the bridge is about to be closed for the passing of trains.

Masters and Pilots are not allowed to sail through the opening of the bridge, but must bring their vessels up to the proper mooring buoys provided for that purpose, and there remain until the signal is exhibited, as above, that the bridge is open, when they must warp their vessels through." Owing to lack of use, the lights were abolished in 1950, as they were not a legal requirement.

76. The lower parts of the trestles of the 1000 foot long bridge had been cased with concrete between 1928 and 1930. After removal of the superstructure the local authority tried unsuccessfully to remove the stumps with explosives in 1973. The new road bridge in the background was opened on 10th September 1956, five months ahead of schedule. Railwaymen continued to collect tolls at it, on behalf of Hampshire County Council, until 11th April 1960. (S.C. Nash)

NORTH HAYLING

77. A northbound train slows down ready to stop at this remote station on the western shore of the Island. North Hayling and Langston were often described as Halts, but tickets and timetables indicated that they were both stations and most trains stopped in any case. However, a new enamel sign "North Hayling Halt" was made in 1949 but it remained in store at Havant until after the branch closed. It was 15ft long and 18ins wide. (Lens of Sutton)

78. Minimal accommodation was provided for passengers but at least they were informed of the fares and train times to Havant in 1963. Tickets were issued by the guard from a hand-held rack. (A.A.F. Bell)

79. A westerly gale at this exposed location takes the excess steam away horizontally and forces a lady's skirt between her legs. Midwinter? No – 28th July 1956. (J.H. Aston)

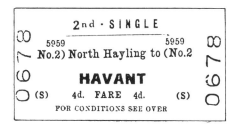

Bradshaw 1910

Miles	Up.							Week Days.												
	HAYLING ISLAND and HAVANT—(Motor Cars—One class only).—L. B. & S. C.																			
		mrn	mrn	mrn	mrn	aft	aft	aft	aft	aft	aft	aft	aft							
	Hayling Island ....dep.	7 55	8 50	9 37	1053	1230	1 20	2 55	4 45	5 50	7 0	8 35	9 45							
2	North Hayling	8 0	8 55	9 42	1058	1235	1 25	3 0	4 50	5 55	7 5	8 40	9 50							
3¼	Langston	8 6	9 1	9 48	11 4	1241	1 31	3 6	4 56	6 1	7 11	8 46	9 56							
4¼	Havant 139, 142, 187 ...arr.	8 10	9 5	9 52	11 8	1245	1 35	3 10	5 0	6 5	7 15	8 50	10 0							

Miles	Down.							Week Days.												
	HAVANT and HAYLING ISLAND—(Motor Cars—One class only).—L. B. & S. C.																			
		mrn	mrn	mrn	non	aft	aft	aft	aft	aft	aft	aft								
	Havant ....dep.	8 20	9 17	1033	12 0	1258	1 50	4 15	5 30	6 25	7 35	9 20								
1	Langston	8 24	9 21	1037	12 4	1 2	1 54	4 19	5 34	6 29	7 39	9 24								
2¼	North Hayling	8 30	9 27	1043	1210	1 8	2 0	4 25	5 30	6 35	7 45	9 30								
4¼	Hayling Island ....arr.	8 35	9 32	1048	1215	1 13	2 5	4 30	5 35	6 40	7 50	9 35								

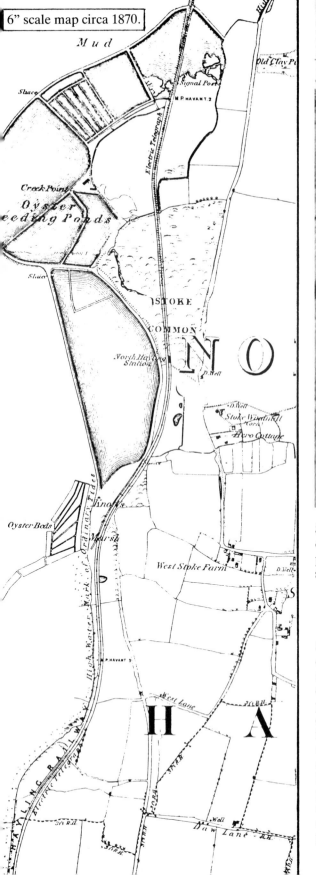

6" scale map circa 1870.

80. In contrast, August Bank Holiday Sunday morning in 1962 brought Hayling-bound passengers onto the tiny platform in short sleeved shirts. (A.A.F. Bell)

→

82. A photograph intended to portray the desolate location of this station. It was taken at the site of a former siding provided for oyster traffic. By 1868 the natural oyster population around the Island had been dredged to near-extinction by vessels from as far afield as Colchester. Following a French example, the first British oyster beds were successfully established on 900 acres of mudland at this location and large tonnages of the palatable bivalve were transported by rail, often to Whitstable. This is another example of an industry developing as a result of the presence of a railway. (A.A.F. Bell)

81. One oil lamp was deemed sufficient for this railway outpost. Guard Norris is seen putting it in place ready for the short dark evening of 18th May 1963. Students of the evolution of lighting would have enjoyed an evening excursion – Langston electric, North Hayling oil and Hayling Island gas. Note the ugly lamp bracket on no. 46, less obvious in other photographs. (A.A.F. Bell)

HAYLING ISLAND

83. The terminus had been called SOUTH HAYLING until 1892. The Gothic style building was designed by F. Whitaker and incorporated timber framing with inset red and white herring-bone brickwork. On the extreme right can be seen the former Petworth engine shed. The locomotive is the Sharp-Stewart 2–4–0T *Hayling Island* described earlier. Local informants indicate that the man by the fence is the Royal Hotel

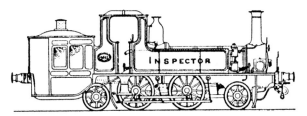

coachman, the top hat is worn by the station master, the light-coloured trousers by the permanent way inspector and that the guard is standing next to the lad by the engine. (National Railway Museum)

RAILWAY STATION. SOUTH HAYLING.

BURROW

BURROW. PUBLISHER. CHELTENHAM

84. The Hampshire Telegraph of April 1st 1899 reported on a meeting between a deputation of local dignitaries and the General Manager of the LBSCR. The deputation asked that provision be made for two trains to stand in the platform at the same time, and that a canopy be provided. These requests were considered to be reasonable and the General Manager promised to submit plans.

The deputation were also told of plans to build a large goods shed. This Burrows coloured postcard clearly shows the canopy and new brick-built goods shed. It is interesting to note that it is still shown as Railway Station, South Hayling, even though the name had been changed to Hayling Island some years earlier. The date is probably Whit Monday 1904. (D. Wallis collection)

85. The station approach about 1910. The then fairly new ticket office extension can be clearly seen at the rear of the original building. The end wall has also had to receive some modification by the addition of large

slates to combat the damp. Several horse-drawn vehicles appear to have arrived in time to meet the train, the vehicle on the extreme left being the Royal Hotel bus.
(C. Fry collection)

HAYLING ISLAND RAILWAY STATION 7616

HAYLING ISLAND. L.B.S.C.R.

86. An early staff portrait taken about 1907, after the construction of the bay to the west side of the platform. (Lens of Sutton)

87. 'The Station, Hayling', another picture postcard taken in the early 1900s. The large slates on the end wall have now been replaced by tiles. Around the turn of the century Hayling had become very popular. (Lens of Sutton)

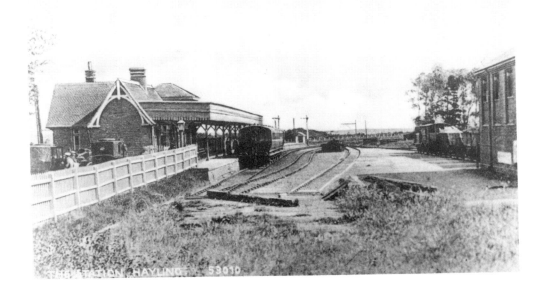

Hayling Island

88. An early photograph, published by E. Pouteau of Grays Inn Road, London, showing the modest coaling stage. The neat appearance of the trackwork suggests that the photograph was taken soon after the yard was rearranged in 1900. (E.R. Lacey collection)

89. The Wallis & Steevens steam roller purchased by the LBSCR in 1901 and photographed in Hayling goods yard in 1933. It was painted umber and fitted with a copper chimney cap. (O.J. Morris/Lens of Sutton)

90. The entire train crew enjoy the tranquill-ity of a Southern branch line terminus whilst a boy examines the punched leather strap of a carriage drop light. The end window of the coach was probably once used for motor-train working. (Lens of Sutton)

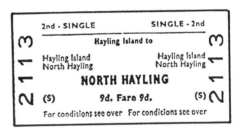

1910 25" scale map.

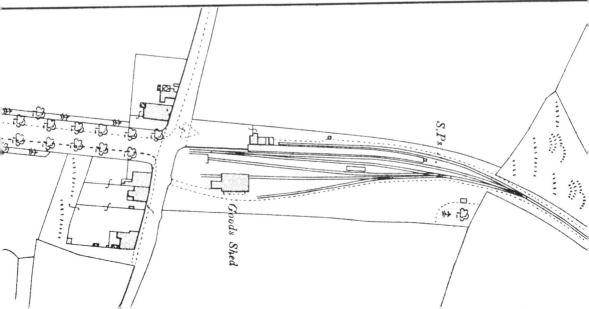

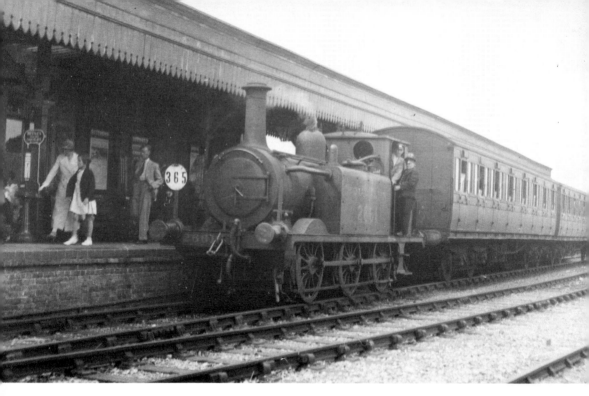

91. An almost timeless Southern view, taken on 21st June 1936. Note the misalignment of engine and train buffers, the roster number on the headcode and the Nestles slot machine on the platform offering chocolate for 1d. (S.W. Baker)

92. A familiar sight in the goods yard for several post war years was this ex-LSWR Fruit Van, with sliding doors and oil lighting. It was used by Landers, a local builders merchant, for the storage of cement. (J.H. Aston)

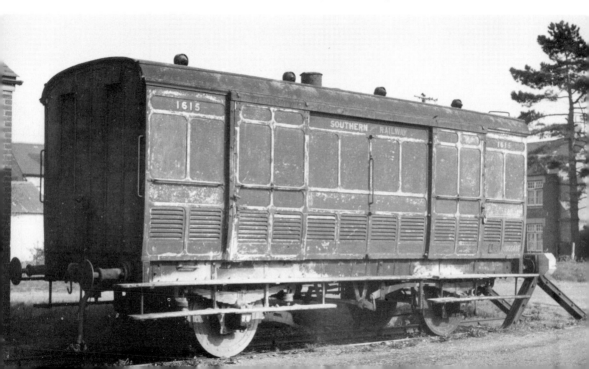

93. No. 55 stands near the goods yard neck with the open fields of Hayling in the distance. No one could have foreseen the fame that this locomotive would later achieve as *Stepney the Bluebell Engine*, immortalised by the Rev. Awdry in his children's books. (E.R. Lacey collection)

94. No. 59 passes the down Home signals in
August 1949 wearing the wartime unlined
black livery with "Sunshine" lettering. The
signal on the left is the Up Advanced Starter.
(S.C. Nash)

PORTSMOUTH, HAVANT, & HAYLING.

London, Brighton, and South Coast.

Town Station,	mrn	mrn	mrn	aft	aft	aft	aft
Portsmouth ..dep	9 0	9 55	1135	1 25	3 25	4 45	7 15
Havant........ "	9 20	1030	1155	2 5	4 10	6 25	7 35
Langston.........	9 24	1034	1159	2 9	4 14	6 29	7 39
North Hayling	9 31	1041	12 6	2 16	4 21	6 36	7 46
South Hayling arr	9 40	1050	1215	2 25	4 30	6 45	7 55
	mrn	mrn	mrn	aft	aft	aft	aft
South Hayling dep	8 5	9 45	1058	1 20	3 10	4 40	6 55
North Hayling.....	8 12	9 52	11 2	1 27	3 17	4 47	7 2
Langston.........	8 19	9 59	11 9	1 34	3 24	4 54	7 9
Havant 70.53. 64 a	8 25	10 5	1115	1 40	3 30	5 0	7 15
Portsmouth 47 "	9 25	1040	12 22	2 16	4 23	5 44	7 33

Bradshaw 1890

L. B. & S. C. Ry

HAYLING ISLAND

To

Portsmouth Harbr

1s.0½d.   Third Cl.   1s.0½d.

See Back

2161   2161

95. In the winter of 1946 austerity conditions made one coach sufficient for the light traffic. The canopy in front of the station building had been rendered unsafe by a bomb blast during the war and was never replaced. During the blackout flares were lit on Hayling to act as a decoy for Portsmouth, inviting the enemy to drop its bombs in the Hayling fields instead of on the city. (A.A.F. Bell)

97. On 12th May 1956, the 12.55 departure was hauled by the familiar no. 40. The 1900 platform extension never received a tarmac surface and so its boundary coincided with the end of the gravelled area. (R.J. Buckley/H.C. Casserley)

HAYLING ISLAND,

Fares—1st, 11/9; 2nd, 7/6; 3rd, 5/10½. Return—1st, 20/3; 2nd, 13/-; 3rd, 11/6.

42 miles from Brighton and 74½ from Tunbridge Wells. The modest little watering-place of South Hayling—which is probably unsurpassed for its grand expanse of firm sand, magnificent sea-views over the anchorage of Spithead to the verdant shores of the Isle of Wight, pure invigorating air, and rural inland scenery—has during late years become most popular with those who prefer the restful quiet of a seaside village to the ceaseless bustle of a fashionable nineteenth-century resort. Excellent bathing and rural rambles, with the advantages of bracing muscular exercise afforded by two golfing clubs respectively for ladies and gentlemen, are amongst the many advantages gained by a sojourn in what may be termed the smallest marine resort in Hampshire. Good bathing is to be had on a sandy beach. A telegraph office will be found at the railway station, and an omnibus meets the trains. Hotel—The "Royal."

---

96. Between 1934 and 1951 railway passengers could continue their journey on route 46. This Leyland TDI of 1929 was operating from Eastoke (A.A.F. Bell)

98. No. 40 brings in the second train of the day on the August Bank Holiday of 1962. After the third train had arrived over 1500 tickets had been collected! (A.A.F. Bell)

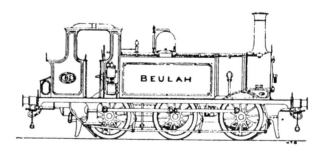

BEULAH

100. The 2.58 pm starts away on 18th February 1963 but Guard Norris is still on the platform. The reason is that it is to be a mixed train. The Guard has left his shunting pole leaning against the empty coal wagon, ready to couple it to the back of the coaches after Driver Beard has reversed the train onto it. Note that the Up Main Starter is a SR-style rail built signal post, but the bay retains its LBSCR tapered wooden post. (A.A.F. Bell)

99. Taken a few minutes after the previous picture, we see the guard about to board the first up train. As soon as it had left, no. 40 would run round its train and transfer it to the bay platform to await departure time, thus leaving the main platform clear for the next arrival. This procedure was employed on all busy days when the 30-minute interval service was operated. (A.A.F. Bell)

101. In the corner of the signal box was an antiquated telephone, an exposed gas mantle and the obligatory train register. At this windy location the latter required a paper-weight. For this purpose an enterprising railwayman had acquired a lavatory door handle from a passing corridor train. (A.A.F. Bell)

⟶

102. The signalman at Hayling Island was a busy man when the ½-hourly summer services were in operation. Apart from the No. 1 Road Down Home Signal (shown here with lever collars on) all 9 levers were operated between the arrival of a down train, the departure of an up train and the 'Road Set' for the next down train. This demanded 36 lever movements in all, 35 in the Signal Box plus one on the spring point at the end of the line. Apart from that, each engine had to be uncoupled and recoupled at least once, plus shunting operations on weekdays. The Tyers One Wire Two Position Block Instruments were in use for the greater part of the line's existence. (A.A.F. Bell)

103. Everything in miniature – the locomotive, the signal box and the mess room. Outside the latter can be seen the loco crew washing facilities – just a bowl on a metal stand! (A.A.F. Bell)

105. Photographed on 2nd March 1963 from the end-loading dock, we see no. 78 approaching the spring loaded points. The signalman is about to jump off so that he can reset the points after the passing of the engine. (A.A.F. Bell)

←

104. Doug Todd adopts a special stance ready to receive the staff from the driver of the second down train on 23rd June 1963. Friendly gestures from engine crews included dipping the end of the staff in oil or pre-heating it in the firebox. Only two minutes was available before the departure of the next up train from the bay. An empty coach was often stored at the end of the bay so that it could easily be attached to the train if traffic demanded it. (A.A.F. Bell)

106. The interior of the 1900 goods shed, through which all but bulk local merchandise would have passed for many years. The hand-operated crane had a lifting capacity of 30cwt. Note the impressive trusses of this well-built structure. In 1963, it was used for the storage of wool and cement. Later, after the Torrey Canyon disaster, the Local Authority stored anti-pollution materials in it. (A.A.F. Bell)

107. Driver Beard and his fireman together with Signalman Todd and Guard Instrall enjoy their break on a bright June morning in 1963. Behind them is one of the standard BR compartment coaches, capable of quicker loading and unloading than corridor coaches. (A.A.F. Bell)

108. Clerk/porter Ray Woolgar exclaims, "what do you mean, you didn't have time to get any tickets?" Yet another delay on a busy day in June 1963. In the background is the spare coach in the bay and the loading gauge in the goods yard. (A.A.F. Bell)

109. The action is seen from the top of No. 2 Road Up Starting Signal on 1st September 1963. The 12.20 (non-stop Havant) is about to leave from no. 1 road whilst the engine of the 12.18 arrival is already waiting on the loop. Idle engine crews sometimes practised "cricket" with a firing shovel and pieces of ballast, which may account for the broken signal box window. (A.A.F. Bell)

110. Contrary to popular belief, double heading was allowed by the Rule Book. Putting two engines onto the 9.14 am from Havant on Saturdays was a convenient way of one engine reaching its train if it had been left in the bay. More commonly, the engines would be at opposite ends of the down train. The trailer on the platform belonged to the local fishmonger. The carriage of fish boxes on passenger trains often left a curious smell in guards vans. (A.A.F. Bell)

111. After working the 6.30 am mixed train from Havant on 7th September 1963, no. 50 ran round its train, removed the goods portion and took it beyond the top points. The locomotive was then uncoupled and it gave the wagons a hefty shove. They continued under their own momentum into the siding, the guard applying the brake in the van when necessary. (A.A.F. Bell)

112. The passengers plod off and the pipe smoker ponders the Closure Notice, all unaware of the camera on the roof. The end loading dock could have been used for the horse-drawn carriages of the gentry in the early years and by the Army in later years. It was also useful for agricultural equipment arriving by rail. (A.A.F. Bell)

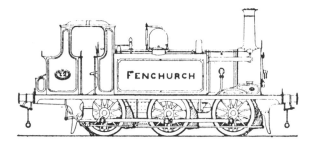

113. The copse has grown considerably since the earlier photographs were taken but otherwise little has changed, except that sleepers have largely disappeared under ash and coal dust. Double door 20-ton wagons were often used for loco coal. Its white diagonal indicated that it also had an end opening door. (A.A.F. Bell)

1948

	HAVANT and HAYLING ISLAND																													
Miles	**Down**	**Week Days**																								**Sundays**					
		a.m	a.m	a.m	a.m	a.m		p.m	p.m	p.m	S O	p.m	p.m	p.m	S X	S O	S X	S O	S X	S O	a.m	a.m		p.m	p.m	p.m	p.m	p.m	p.m	p.m
	Havant .... dep	6 35	7 17	8 16	9 7	10 19	11 19	..	12 6	12 50	1 34	2 20	3 53	4 25	5 20	6 34	7 20	7 54	8 20	8 34	10 35	11 35	..	12 35	1 35	2 35	3 35	5 35	6 35	7 35	..
1	Langston	6 38	7 23	8 19	9 10	10 22	11 22	..	12 9	12 53	1 37	2 23	3 56	4 55	5 36	6 23	6 37	7 23	7 37	8 23	8 37	10 38	11 38	..	12 38	1 38	2 38	3 38	5 38	6 38	7 38
2¾	North Hayling	..	7 29	8 23	9 16	10 25	11 26	..	12 13	12 57	1 41	2 27	4 0	4 49	5 40	6 27	6 41	7 27	7 41	8 27	8 41	10 42	11 42	..	12 42	1 42	2 42	3 42	5 42	6 42	7 42
4½	Hayling Island .... arr	6 45	7 35	8 29	9 22	10 32	11 32	..	12 19	1 3	1 47	2 33	4 6	4 55	5 46	5 33	6 47	7 33	7 47	8 33	8 47	10 48	11 48	..	12 48	1 48	2 48	3 48	5 48	6 48	7 48

S O Saturdays only.   S X Saturdays excepted.

	HAYLING ISLAND and HAVANT																													
Miles	**Up**	**Week Days**																					**Sundays**						
		a.m	a.m	a.m	a.m	a.m	a.m		p.m	p.m	S O	S X	S O	p.m	p.m	p.m	p.m	p.m				a.m	a.m		p.m	p.m	p.m	p.m	p.m	p.m	p.m
	Hayling Island .... dep	6 58	7 46	8 40	9 45	1052	11 45	..	12 27	1 12	1 57	3 18	3 22	4 16	5	6 5	5 57	6 52	7 52	8 52	..	1055	1155	..	1255	1 55	2 55	4 55	5 55	6 55	7 55
1¾	North Hayling	7 2	7 50	8 44	9 49	1056	11 49	..	12 31	1 16	2 1	3 24	3 26	4 20	5 10	6	1 6	5 57	6 56	8 56	..	1059	1159	..	1259	1 59	2 59	4 59	5 59	6 59	7 59
3¾	Langston	7 7	7 55	8 49	9 54	11 1	11 54	..	12 36	1 21	2 6	3 30	3 31	4 25	5 15	6	6 7	1 8	1 9	1	..	11 4	12 4	..	1 4	2 4	3 4	5 4	6 4	7 4	8 4
4½	Havant 159, 196, 366 ... arr	7 13	7 f 9	8 55	8 59	11 5	11 58	..	12 40	1 25	2 10	3 35	3 35	4 29	5 19	6	10 7	5 8	5 9	5	..	11 8	12 8	..	1 8	2 8	3 8	5 8	6 8	7 8	8 8

S O Saturdays only   S X Saturdays excepted

115. Loading one of the "flats" on the last day of services are Messrs. Ripsher, Evans, Nash and Instrall. The perforated leather strap referred to earlier is now visible. (A.A.F. Bell)

114. Harry and Ray were about to lose their local taxi work but they would be making more journeys to Havant in future. The gas lamp is the *Rochester* model, made by Messrs Sugg of Westminster. (A.A.F. Bell)

116. Relief signalman Herbert Brooke prepares to couple up to the last empty coal wagon on 2nd November 1963, leaving enough coal on the stage for the last day. The remaining wagons, loaded with railway enthusiasts, formed an early evening mixed train which started from the bay platform. (A.A.F. Bell)

118. After services ceased, nature soon took over but Station Stores continued to proudly use that name. All the railway property was acquired by Havant & Waterloo U.D.C. which later became the Borough of Havant. (Lens of Sutton)

117. The outer office during the last week of operation with the ticket rack visible through the window to the inner office. The handbill rack is nearly empty but souvenir photographs by A.A.F. Bell and Christmas cards were on sale. (A.A.F. Bell)

119. Before the line closed, the Hayling Light Railway Society was formed. It proposed the overhead electrification of the route and the operation of tramcars. This ex-Blackpool Corporation car, no. 11 built in 1939, was acquired and remained in Havant goods yard until the scheme foundered, due partly to the proposed bypass. The car was moved to the East Anglian Museum of Transport in 1969. (E. Wilmshurst)

120. Although the station buildings were demolished, the canopy was dismantled and has been re-erected to serve steam trains once again. They run on the two-foot gauge line of the Hollycombe Steam Collection, two miles south of Liphook, which is open to visitors on summer week-ends. The locomotive on the passenger train is a rare Barclay 0–4–0 WT named *Caledonia*. (J.M. Baldock collection)